ISBN 1 871964 01 6

Illustrations and Cover design by Ian Churchill,

Printed in Great Britain.

. . .OF COURSE I LOVE YOU

Ideas Unlimited (Publishing)

Many thanks to Ian Churchill for his brilliant illustrations without which this book would be meaningless.

CONTENTS

A MESSAGE TO THE ONE I LOVE

SEE PAGE. . . . .

FROM THE ONE YOU LOVE

8

DON'T YOU KNOW. . . . . . ?

That love means never having to say the words "I LOVE YOU". Never having to question, analyse or even try to explain those intimate feelings. For doing so, may entail disastrous consequences.

You see, for the precious time that I have known you, I have stored up the hurts, tolerated your annoying habits, and have had to keep a brave and happy face throughout. Yet you still insist on asking me the unbearable question:

"DO YOU LOVE ME?"

All I can say to that, my sweet heart, is:

"OF COURSE I LOVE YOU"

I love you despite the fact that you are who you are, what you are, and how you are.

I love. . . .

I love the way you always make me feel so very special.

I love the way you always make me feel so proud to introduce you as the man of my dreams.

I love the way you always make me feel like your one and only pride and joy.

I love the way you make an effort to try and get on with my friends.

I love the clever little ways you try to protect me from getting hurt.

Oh hello darling, come in, I was just interviewing the new Nanny!

19

I love the romantic outings you take me on.

21

In times of danger, I can always count on you to act quickly and do the right thing.

23

24

I love your cute wondering eyes, and the discreet way you use them.

I love the romantic evenings we spend together,

We always share the happy times

. . . .And we share the sad times.

You are so thoughtful. . . .getting things done quickly so that I can get my beauty sleep.

I love the way you try to keep me busy, tidying up after you.
. . So that I would never get bored.

You are so perceptive and never miss a trick.

You mean I am going to be a daddy?

I love your tact, subtlety and understanding; particularly when it comes to my little weaknesses.

Of course the earth moved for me, darling.

Of course you are the only one in my life, darling.

41

TEST 1

He comes home drunk, trousers torn, shirt hanging out, covered with lip stick and stinking of cheap perfume. Would you:

a) Welcome him home with love and affection, tell him how much you missed him, carry him to bed and cuddle up to him all night.

b) Knock him unconscious, burn off the lipstick marks off his face, dismantle one or two parts of his body, which would not only prevent him from ever doing that again, but would also prevent him from even having the desire to.

c) Just let it go, and be glad that at least one of you had a good time that evening.

43

TEST 2

You suspect him of having an affair. Would you:

a) Pull out every single hair on his body, one by one, slowly, until he tells you the truth. Then after the confession, transplant them back with a blunt needle.

b) Kill him for just giving you cause to be suspicious, and then find out the truth later through other means such as autopsy etc.

c) Forgive him for these things happen.

45

TEST 3

Bless his little soul, he has forgotten your birthday, would you:

a) Tattoo your date of birth on his forehead, preferably with a blunt instrument, so that there is no chance of it ever happening again.

b) Light the candles on your cake, take them off and stick them up his nose one by one, helping his brain to associate the event with a slight burning feeling up his nose, which would almost certainly prevent him from ever forgetting again.

c) Forgive him this time, but if he forgets next year, make sure that the candles will be the extra large ones, and they would certainly not be aimed at his nose.

TEST 4

The love of your life has a slight social problem. . . B.O., would you:

a) Learn to love it as you would the most expensive French perfume.

b) Tell him straight that he is a stinking little skunk, and unless he began to smell more human, you would leave him as he deserves to be left.

c) Take the more subtle route of opening an account with the main suppliers of soaps, deodorants etc. in the district.

49

TEST 5

having a drink with a few friends, you suddenly notice that his fly is undone. Would you:

a) Tell your friends and have a good laugh about it before telling him.

b) Tell your friends and have a good laugh about it, but don't let him find out what everyone has been grinning about all evening.

c) Drop subtle hints about flying in the hope that he gets the message before anyone else.

51

RESULTS

Test 1:	Test 2:
a) 5 points	a) 5 points
b) 3 points	b) 7 points
c) 7 points	c) 3 points

Test 3:	Test 4:
a) 5 points	a) 3 points
b) 7 points	b) 7 points
c) 3 points	c) 5 points

Test 5:

a) 5 points   b) 7 points
c) 3 points

If you have scored:

0-20	Hopeless love affair
21-25	Fairly good love affair
26 and above	You two were made for each other

...OF COURSE I LOVE YOU

Boy to Girl

I love the Saturday outings you take me on, every week.

55

I love the sweet way you prefer to communicate without using a single word.

I try to appreciate your love of the arts, don't I?

You are so understanding, particularly when it comes to my little weaknesses.

You certainly know how to make a very long wait seem worth – while.

63

I love your hormones, and the cute way they change; giving rise to those subtle little changes in your mood.

. . .I always compliment you on your figure, don't I?

68

You will always be high on my list, even amongst the most attractive of creatures.

I Love those subtle little hints you drop, when it comes to planning our future.

I love the little surprises you always spring on me.

I love the way you always make other guys so envious of me!

I love the subtle little hints you drop to tell me you are not in the mood.

I love your managerial skills, particularly the way you delegate work.

I love the way you always make my friends feel welcome.

I even love the little differences of opinion we occasionally have.

One day off a week, and I still spend it with the family. Don't I?

TEST 1

Twenty minutes into the first half of the Cup Final, she suddenly tells you that she is in love with someone else. Would you:

a) Wait till the match is over, then discuss it.

b) Wait till the half time and try to discuss it before the second half starts.

c) Pretend your didn't hear her until the end of the game, then kill her.

TEST 2

She crashes your brand new car before you have had the chance to insure her. Would you:

a) Kill her.

b) Kill her slowly.

c) Or go easy on her by just making her repair the body work with her bare teeth.

TEST 3

She has just come back from the girl's room, her skirt tucked in her pants. Would you:

a) Shout it out and let everyone have a good laugh.

b) Tell everyone quietly, and have a good laugh.

c) Don't say anything, just point and let everyone have a good laugh.

TEST 4

You want a cuddle, but she has a headache. Would you:

a) Sit and sulk.

b) Take a cold shower, then sit and sulk.

c) Sooth her headache with some relaxing music. Perhaps a loud heavy metal track.

TEST 5

She has just bought a new dress which looks hideous on her. Would you:

a) Tell her that she looks sensational in it.

b) Tell her that she has never looked so beautiful.

c) Arrange to accidentally destroy the dress beyond recognition later.

RESULTS

Test 1:	Test 2:
a) 3 points	a) 5 points
b) 5 points	b) 7 points
c) 7 points	c) 2 points

Test 3:	Test 4:
a) 7 points	a) 5 points
b) 5 points	b) 7 points
c) 3 points	c) 3 points

Test 5:

a) 7 points   b) 5 points

c) 3 points

SCORES:

Below 20	Hopeless love affair
21-25	Fairly good love affair
26 and above	You two were made for each other.

OTHER TITLES AVAILABLE FROM IDEAS UNLIMITED (PUBLISHING).

Please send me:

- [ ] copy / copies of **"100 Chat Up Lines"** ISBN 1-871964-00-8 (128 pages A7) — @ **£1.99** (postage free)
- [ ] copy / copies of **"Of course I Love You"** ISBN 1-871964-01-6 (96 pages A6) — @ **£1.99** (postage free)
- [ ] copy / copies of **"The Beginners Guide to Kissing"** ISBN 1-871964-02-4 (64 pages A5) — @ **£2.50** (postage free)
- [ ] copy / copies of **"Tips for a Successful Marriage"** ISBN 1-871964-03-2 (64 pages A5) — @ **£2.50** (postage free)
- [ ] copy / copies of **"The Joy of Fatherhood"** ISBN 1-871964-04-0 (64 pages A5) — @ **£2.50** (postage free)
- [ ] copy / copies of **"Office Hanky Panky"** ISBN 1-871964-05-9 (64 pages A5) — @ **£2.50** (postage free)

I Have enclosed a cheque / postal order for £............................ made payable to Ideas Unlimited (Publishing)

Name: ....

Address: ....

Fill in the coupon and send it with your payment to: **Ideas Unlimited (Publishing) PO Box 125, Portsmouth PO1 4PP**